We All Come from Somewhere

Amy Edelstein

ISBN: 0-9969285-1-0
ISBN 13:   978-0-9969285-1-9

For more on Amy Edelstein's work and publications from
Emergence Education Press:

www.EmergenceEducationPress.com
www.AmyEdelstein.com

*For my mother whose perseverance
in so many ways fueled my own quest*

*And for Theodore Roethke, William Carlos Williams, &
Adrienne Rich
whose words were my best companions when I first started
to wake up*

We All Come from Somewhere is a collection of poems I began when the poet's itch reawakened in me some thirty years after a long quiet spell. They are immediate and very personal poems, stories of my life and memories, incidents working their way through me, and a voice for a narrative I rarely share. They are not necessarily the poems I wanted to write; they are the poems that wanted to be written first. I hope through the personal, you find the universal, that through the shadows and half shapes, you find mystical presence. Through my story may you find more about me as well as more about you, about the world, and about the fragmented human experience as it happens, as we work our way back or forward toward a narrative of the One.

Amy Edelstein
Philadelphia, PA
January 2016

Contents

Stories to Tell   1

Old Indian Country   3

It's Your Lucky Day   7

Beyond the Self Same Things   13

What We Say   19

Fourth Element   20

You Will See   23

Connecting with What's There   24

Before We Thought We Knew   26

Seventeen   30

In the Lineage   36

Memories   39

Walk-in   40

Getting On the Inside   43

Dreams

    i. The Forming   46

    ii. The Promise   48

    iii. The Meantime   51

    iv. The Coda   52

    v. The Requiem   54

Refusing to be Finished   57

Stories to Tell

We all have stories to tell
How easy it is to see the story
In the other, in the negress
With her tiny wizened face, mother just shy
of one hundred and five
Grew up in a two-bedroom house
Not much more than a shack, the walls so thin
Wind whistled through
Oh yeah, she's got a story to tell.

Or the self-made man
With three lovely daughters,
All ready to be married
With dreams of their own
Under his approving eye
Beats a heart open as a watermelon smile
All broad and semi-circled and toothy.

We all want each other
to tell our stories
for us
Making them shine

like shells buffed by the salt-turquoise sea
Special secretive instructive treasures.

It's hard to begin
unraveling the skein of our own narrative
rather put it back in its drawer
for another time
instead
tell a story for its own sake
to the cat, curing on the radiator
who might just listen to us
and purr.

Old Indian Country

I.

Massapequa

Saginaw

Patchogue

Roll these names off your tongue

as you walk among the reeds at the side of the bay

Inverted paintbrushes dancing in the crisp of morning

blending mediums

Like Diaghilev's ballet in the twenties

Art and nature both seek for embodied expression—

The hopes and dreams of a new year—

the immediacy of today.

I love this land.

It reminds me of something more than my history

my memories—

I love it with a fierce heart,

alone, no one telling me to,

open, no one telling me how to.

II.

Outside my window the birchbark flaps in the wind

Almost blood orange, feathering out from a slender
trunk
Like sheet parchment
Waiting for the inked quill.
The Indigenous tell stories
Long and meandering
If you have all day to wait for the chapter's end

If I had money, first
I would buy tons of land
Beautiful land with waterheads
Like Robert Redford in the seventies
On that land I would let beauty be or make beauty
Where urbanity sat
And see what that does for our future.

III.
Right now out in the garden
The cold rhododendron leaves paddle in the breeze
Sweeping up the sun in big flat strokes
Tipping it over and tumbling it down
What an efficient little paddlewheel
Scooping and paddling, scooping and paddling,
backlit, playing movement with the wind.

Sometimes I wonder if that is all I do
If there is bigger purpose in my paddling
Scooping the light that shines from behind
Pouring it up over me
So it rolls down and licks at my skin
My offering of Self back
when it gives anyway
always unstintingly

IV.
In this old Indian country
In the morning, even not too early
You can feel the old soul of the land
With its ballads and histories
Its myths and paths
Earth has a way of being moral
Without harshness
Of being instructive
Without narrating
Of comforting
Without taking away the aloneness.

If I had the means
I would go to the reservations

And start retelling the beauty of place to the teens
Get them to dig up the stories
Scratch beneath the surface
For tubers and bulbs
And find the poems of the land.

If there were but one thing that
can heal the hidden sorrows
It's the stories of the earth
Where we always find One
Where we always find home.

It's Your Lucky Day
for Joe

"It's your lucky day,"
Joe said to me.
He was young and handsome
In that rough woodsy way.
I knew him only
Vaguely. At the moment when he told me
It's your lucky day
I didn't even know I knew him.
To me, he wasn't Joe, he was an angel.

Joe worked as an occasional groundsman
Where I worked as an assistant.
One of my jobs, after twenty-five years of executive
level experience
Was to shoo away distractions for the prince, sort of a
reverse Siddhartha,
In more ways than one.
It was Joe's job one day
To trim the tall hedges that ran all the way round the
estate
So it was my job to nicely

Ask him to stop doing his job, so the reverse prince
could eat his sandwich
And talk on the phone without minor discomforts of
any kind.
Such was the backdrop of when I first met Joe.

Joe was one of those people who sort of drifted
In and out
Not in a vagrant kind of way
Just like dandelion fur
That hasn't yet tumbled to its home.
Joe had that knack of mysteriously being
in the right place
At the right time
Almost as if he was an apparition or walked in barefoot
And silent like an Indian tracker.

Actually of all places,
Joe was on his way to a sweat lodge
With some friends somewhere out near Egremont in
the woods
a self made lodge with bent over saplings and wool
tarps
erected by hand and dismantled the same day
That's why he was where he was,

In that clear patch at the crook
of the country road.
To him it was ordinary,
But to me it was all too coincidental
That's why I think Joe is an angel
Even though to Joe, he is just Joe.

You see, when I opened my eyes
After a big bang
I saw Joe standing a little way off
Turned a little way towards or away from
I couldn't quite tell—
I could sort of see him out of the corner of my eye
In the dusk and the mist
Not really see him, but sort of.
I thought I asked him, "Can you help me?"
But it might have just been my own voice
In my own head.
Then there he was
And he did.

No time passed before his warm rough hands
were cradling my wet, sticky neck,
Each big paw-palm wrapping its way under each ear

Almost up to my forehead, almost down to my
shoulders
All the while, saying in a low voice,
"It's your lucky day, it's your lucky day."

I don't know how
he knew just what to do
He must have been reaching through
from the back
I thought he was inside, right with me
I could feel his heart and body beating
Beating life into mine

Joe wasn't telling me something he wanted me to
believe
He was telling me something
he already knew was true
And so I knew it too.

Joe was with me
It seemed like eternity
    and then he wasn't.
It got very busy all of a sudden
I think I saw him watching from about ten feet away
I think I saw him through a part in the crowds

Then the rain took over
The task at hand took over
Life took over.

I heard he was telling his friend Dave the next day
what he saw,
Dave said, Last night?
Don't you know?
That was our gal.
Joe was surprised
in the way I think he might often be
When he appears
Just when you need him
And not longer.

He came to see me once
In my convalescent apartment on the ground floor
I wanted to thank him
Later I bought him a photograph of a sunlight field and
I titled it
It's Your Lucky Day
But I never found him, no one seemed to quite know
where he was
though he was
Around

I hope Joe knows I think
he's really an angel
And if he doesn't want to be found out
that's ok with me.
I'm happy for everyone else that Joe will happen to be
there
Just when they need it to say
It's your lucky day
Hang on.

Beyond the Self Same Things

For Jesmyn Ward and Ta-Nehisi Coates

I wake up these mornings
With a tightness in my belly
And a watchfulness, listening to the scratchings
voices from the past
The voices of history I am not surprised to find
But didn't know were there
Or what they were saying
Before.

Truth sayings
Story sayings
Warning sayings
Witnesses
They roll me one way and the other
Seasick I turn

They draw back veils of mystery and blame
The misunderstandings, not understandings
that separate me from
Separate good neighbors with nice lawns

from razor wire, boarded windows, and sorry plastic
bags hugging chainlink fences
Don't take me away from here.

When I first moved here
I felt embarrassed and sad
Shocked and sad
Bewildered really

Walking at dusk
In my neighborhood
I'd pass a kid and feel
his fear, like a padding
Between him and me
Between hello and me
Hands dug into pockets, eyes downcast
He'd stride by
then exhale
(I'm hardly the threatening type)
In the passing, I'd steal
a glance for eyes
for the youth, the zest, the fun, the free
the hello
Now I don't need to look
I understand.

The truth makes sense.
Without history, without roots
The present is a jumble of unintelligible
disheartening circumstances
That turn against an individual
That separate the ones doing good
From the ones who do not.

There are always causes
That have effects
That's what's called karma.
Until the truth is made known
Karma mostly affects those it touches
Not those who set the waves in motion.
And we know from Katrina waves
Made of such soft and nearly invisible water, raze
with power and wrath.

No, it is always better to have the truth out
Even though truth can be told from many sides
depending on the experiencer
—there's no single objective truth
in spite of what some insist—
Like a kaleidoscope
little mosaic shards fall into a pattern

intelligible and in an order
that makes sense of things.
Look through the viewer and you'll see it too.

I learned through personal experience
That fact, history, causes, is what gives rise to culture
big cultures, microcultures
to anomalies among whole peoples
genders, age groups.
Those behaviors aren't inevitable, they are responses
understandable from the circumstances they arise from.
The opportunities, positive and negative, extended or
denied.
Madiba knew there must be truth
For there to be reconciliation
Ben Gurion knew there must be reparations
To live again in the world.

Never forget means we see in context
Seeing in context we see the long fingers of history
How they dig rivulets in the sand of our lives
Some pool on the peaks
Others tumble into the valleys
Through no fault of their own
Except that that's where history drew the lines.

And history is made by men
And women but mostly men,
Women write the subtext under a narrative men have
formed

We can't change what has been
or blame the heirs and descendants for being formed
and acting out of history
But we all can see the causes, the great winds
blowing on the surface of civilization
fashioning us into the lives we lead now
And find a way through.

And those who have held power
And shaped those lines
Stroked those valleys with their own hands
Must, of anyone, see the self same truth.
In their seeing of the same story
—even from their own point of view—
comes the way to redemption
metamorphosis.

When you see differently, you are no longer the person
Who did those self same things.
Apology is acknowledgement.

The one who acknowledges is no longer,
in some essential way,
The one who perpetrated.

Acknowledgement is tangible
as well as of the heart
Material, that which we can touch and know,
is of essence
meaning it is essential
From that we lay
cornerstones of new history
a history beyond the self-same things,
a history that liberates us all.

What We Say

We say we want to plant seeds
But when the prodigies stray
Too far from the nest
We find it all a little sad.
We turn it back on ourselves
Like the milkweed pod that's opened and sprayed
All its seeds down to the last one
Drying, it arches back on itself
Reaching again toward the open cavern
Aware of the emptiness
Unsure, accepting.
We all have our own
Next step.

Fourth Element

You are wiser than we think
Calmer, cooler, often overlooked
Of all the elements

You shape shift
And we rarely realize you, in all your forms, are one
Flexible and powerful
More of a force and a teacher than we want to know.
Gentle as an infant's bathing pool
Clear as a polished lens
with guppies and fishes darting under rock ledges
Lady turns essence into teeming life.

Just the other side of your stillness
you curl and pound with speed and force
mesmerizing, unrelenting
and dangerous.
You can be wrath
insistent and impatient,
Collapsing at the edges
To draw the shore back into yourself.

Your life exceeds the canyons
Patient as a rivulet,
you cut your mark into curves and valleys
caressing with your inky locks.

Turn away and you've slipped into your cloak winter-
white
Stiff, regal, commanding
And the earth falls hushed
Then you pry open mountainsides
With weight and cunning
Slipping fingers into tiny cracks, exploding
granite faces to buckets of smithereens.

We think of you as no consequence
In our glasses on our lunch tables
Cleaning our teeth or our skin
But you kiss the ether
Hot as sin or clammy as fog
Hiding worlds in your shroud

Oh Lady
Cradle the moon in a single drop
Swallow me whole
Wash me into brilliant color

Fix me into diamantine brilliance
Cover me over space and time
And scatter me across the Universe
So I can too be Life in its most essential form
Patient and ever-ready to transform.

You Will See

melancholy
frozen
winter
gives way
to spring again
So hearts give way to Love
Once more

Believe
Connection is
stronger and more of a statement
than fragmentation
It takes more work
to let go

Let go
for Love
she said
And you will see

Connecting with What's There

When I went home that Saturday
The leaves on the crabapple hung crimson rubbery
After finally the first frost.

It was neither a happy nor a sad time
for myself, though certainly for others
it could be one of either, or both.

We spend too much of our time in categories
That we miss the connection with what's there—
The sun, the crisp air, the caress of a chairback on tired
shoulders.

I see your beard sprouting white
Wiry and thick as it bends its way over your chin.
When do we get old? I for one don't feel it nor do I see
it in you my love

Though now I celebrate children, not my own
Curious fingers gripping a pencil stub so eager to
please,
"Good Morning Miss, may God bless you and keep you"

One girl's mother has just left for good, it was love of
drink
though they all say she also loved her children strong
and true.

In this wide world, it is possible to not fear stepping out
Raising our chest up to meet the sun
Standing as mountain, as star, as tree

We who marry our lives with our path
Surely have a long lead to follow
And an arrival that is always here

Before We Thought We Knew

Before we thought we knew
there stretches an open expanse
blazing
spirit-light
that captures bits of our world
in its sacred melting butter way
the way sun slides through fronds in a Thai jungle,
hot and steamy, orange and yellow
foreign yet somehow close
beautiful and wild
scented with mystery and cinnamon and cardamom and
love.
oh and wholeness
wholeness that reaches out from a child's first set of
teeth
pearls gleaming white, catching that self same sun.

Before we thought we knew a shy smile
steals forward, soul-stretching
its small fingers forward, unfurling its pudgy fist
without yet skills to grasp or hold
just open and trusting and awkward and curious

and delectable and huggable and eatable and kissable
bubbling discovery
joy of the ages
all whirr and rush and feathery rumble
flying and flying
scooping one more catchment of great clear air
and one more
and one
more.
The heights are dizzying,
exhilarating, frightening
power of wing, sinew, muscle, and skin stretching over
swiss-cheese skeleton,
covering distance, painting shadows on marsupials and
muskrats
the little creatures below
with flight and distance and force and current.

God is not meek
God is vast and powerful.
Love is not meek, or hidden or mediocre or tamable
Love is vast and powerful.

Before we thought we knew is an embrace of infinity
a way without twistedness

the power to move fast and quick and strong,
striking ground with trisul
and in that very spot
where point pierces crust
showering a clean spring high into the air
unsullied by minerals and ore
(those are meant to ferment in the belly
of the earth
for far, far longer)
Do you ever ask if you can bosom
not one or ten but
thousands of children? Bring all the refugees home?
And still have home still be as silent and solitary
as the monastery you never went to,
the nunnery that never got built
where you can enfold in a journey
all the way back till connection itself dissolves

Before we thought we knew there were shadows
Brief sun-clouds of angels
freeing all the hostaged hearts
not through psychology or history,
Jubilee kind of free
smoothing the left over marks
we branded ourselves

when we were winding, turning, curling like tendrils on
a vine,
reaching above the canopy of dark
Oh the human pretzels we become
contorting back on ourselves
in our search for higher ground

Before we thought we knew, there were songs
I long for those, for the heart and channel
to talk to the orangutans, to put out the fires in the
peat of their habitat
so they no longer ever burn the soles of their feet.

Seventeen

The Beatles sang about it
Happy and light
To me, seventeen
Was a ticket
Out
The out
Had its own dangers, angers
But the horizon was open
And you could always keep travelling, travelling

Quests are like that
They are sometimes another word
For needing to leave
To reach somewhere else
Not here
And then you make them what you will
You make them
Quests of the grail
To where you always and ever
Are.

He was a silent angry type
Occasionally blowing

Mostly kept under lock and key
As if there were some beautiful terrible treasure
That he wouldn't share
Inside the chest were little boy's toys
Ratted with age and dust
Artifacts from the first years in the New World
that carried for him all of meaning, all of love
The faint shadow of the old country
Still visible in the Los Angeles sun
The soft blur, what was left of what it took to come
here.

They clung to each other, the family that made it over
They made their lives anew
Cars and smiles plastered over
the baggage stickers on a single suitcase
The sadnesses in between the lining
But you could still tell
by their musty smell.

He lived in a past
that never got shared in the present
His anger never made sense
But it was beneath the lining just the same.
She was always trying

To pry under it
To get some relatedness, some response
It never really worked
They weren't close but
they were a couple
all they had was each other.

He travelled so much
To a science lab, dull in its hour after hour wait and
repetition
The thrill for those very few who came on quantum
discoveries
And won international prizes
He ran experiments all night
I imagined they smoked and drank scotch
Like most travelling men in the sixties
I imagined he did what most men did
Though I wouldn't know for sure

Home was stable on the surface
Volcanic underneath
I actually thought ours was a happy one
Even though I was not
Such are the myths we tell ourselves.
One time when I was seventeen

Seventeen going on thirty-five
he slapped me across the face
I remember the smell of the heat, the screaming, the
white hot sweat
The raw rage of a culture and history that was too much
to understand
That was a moment, as they say,
It closed the door on what brought me into this life
And sent me searching
for my life
For that which has no birth
no sadness, no shame.

He wasn't a bad man
But he never grew up
Never wanted to live in the big world
With the big people
You might not be able to see it
But he always carried that trunk
With the artifacts of a little boy
In long shorts and a cap

Once I met a young tulku
In Dharmsala. He wore a black leather jacket
And hung out with the gangs.

What made him a precious one? I wondered
He acted like a punk, a sad but volatile seventeen
Filled with hormones and exile and rage
I heard he'd been recognized before they fled
But his father didn't know and beat him when he was
young
They say he never recovered.
You see, tulkus have very open hearts
They need incredible care when they are young
That's why they are carried on the shoulders
Of loving attendants, their senior in years,
Their junior in rank
Their job, their practice, their renunciation
to honor the precious ones
Play and make them laugh.

I wonder what happened to him, the tulku
The dharma punk
In these last thirty years
Did he recover now?
Or forget?
assimilate the hurt,
assimilate himself?
The world is a vast canvas
And the colors cross its surface quickly, changing fast

Changing hue

Washing saffron with green

Muddying the canvas in its wake

Where will we be in ten, twenty years, generations

And where will be these little boys

With their trunks of old world memories and hurts?

In the Lineage

Whirling, stomping, ecstatic and manic
the newlyweds are actually commanded to let go into a
frenzy
It's part of their preparation
To leave one way of being
and bond in passion and matrimony
A ritual oddly intimate
and distant.

You can't access it from the outside
and to be on the inside
that requires a bloodline and an obeisance
to values long replaced.
Or have they been?
Some young ones retain their innocence

But the nobility with spindly beards
protect each other
to a fault, he told me
Study and integrity
Study and morality
Study and kindness

Don't necessarily go together.
Sad when the DA holds a greater moral code
than these men of the book.

Reuven, who had been a zealot,
Walked out tonight
In the middle of the ceremony.
One of the elders presiding
asked the assembly
To pray for one of their own
Who was ill and they prayed.
He neglected to say, pray for quick healing from this flu
that afflicts him
in prison and may his time there awaken his conscience
and his soul

You see, one parent had finally gone to the DA
Instead of the tribe
Others had been told
A second, third, and more times
We'll take care of it.
Religion and righteousness don't have to go together
Though they should.

I know in my bones how a doctrine calcifies

And makes previously uncomfortable positions
Comfortable, in fact acceptable, positive.
The code separates us
from the context
True mystery gets lost
Drowned by the passion, frenetic heel stomping and
wheeling round and round and round
and round and round.

Memories

The body doesn't lie
It stores memories
We don't always interpret them
Properly but there is a map
To find our way home.
The calf, our ancestors
On our father's side
So much anger both ways
Mistrust
Betrayal
What I thought was there wasn't there
What I thought was depth
Was just brooding silence
Oh so popular
In the *Easy Rider* seventies
All promise no dialogue
There was no bridge, no golden gate
To cross
Just arches in my heart leading away, open to the West
And then the East
Away, for awhile,
Let no one see how naïve I was
To have hoped.

Walk-In

Did you ever live in a place that was so picture perfect
you were afraid to come in
Maybe your shoes were dusty
or your hair unkempt
And you probably had dirt underneath your fingernails
If not today then some other day
making you not quite belong here?
California is like that
Even the town names
Sound oddly inviting and restrictive
Larkspur, Mill Valley, Sausalito, and Tiburon
No matter that Alan Watts made his home around here
And Grace Slick and Gary Snyder and oh so many more

Arriving here, winding up our new street
Canopied and hushed by redwoodsUp and up and up,
till the road finally opened to the sky
kabammmm
There was the mountain smack up against our living
room window.
Stunning, so close, but for the canyon in between
Don't fall

Tamalpais must harken to some ancient roots,
With native tracks, and holy hidden places on the far
side where it shakes its skirts to meet the shore
Now, bikes crisscross its belly
And jaguars crouch at its base
Gleaming chrome and silver and powder blue

Living here was like the mountain, circled in mist
A walk-in people sort of sensed
But never really saw or remembered
Living here seemed only fit for breatharians
Or anyone else who doesn't leave a mark
After a decade, the post office clerk never let on she
knew my name
Even though there were only a few thousand in the
town
And every year, I asked her to save my mail
For a month while I disappeared to the exotic East.
Not recognizing is a subtler form of disapproval
Arguably more effective.

Packing to leave
I breathed big loud gulps of air
As box after box loaded onto the train
My body started rearranging itself

I was mute
But I could feel my roots stirring
Hope stirring
Awkward, like the airplane wheels clanking against
their holds
preparing to extend
on the Eastern runway
Coming home.

Getting on the Inside

It was raining, mid-morning, late autumn. That non-
descript
time of year, time of day, weather
Nothing to distinguish itself from the dreary and
mundane
From the loss of substance, of lifeforce, of purpose,
connection
No hope and not even the tumult of despair
Just grey, light rain, bare Massachusetts' trees waving
their stick fingers
against the dull sky.

Everyone was inside
On the inside inside
Or, the others, just inside the room
Concocting plans and laughter, schemes and ways
they all seemed senseless to me, insignificant, past,
empty
We cannot inject soul
Even into an empty space, soul must seep in on its own.
Or must it?

I read a letter from my lover
It was sad but matter-of-fact
He was going to move on
Tired of waiting in the grey rain
In the mid-morning, in the inbetween season, behind
the wheel
Of my parked car, the mist formed drops on the
windshield
I stayed inside, in the outside, looking out.

There was no drama, no fanfare, no contrived or
constructed urgency
I couldn't craft a perfect tin soldier storm
Looking out in the absence of fanfare, of drama, of tin
soldier storm
I realized, as one realizes when you look at things
again, just looking -

We are all outside, even when we are inside
And we are all inside even when we are outside
My life has never been separate from the inside I was
reaching for
proving myself for
Over my shoulder, looking back

through reams and sheaves of scrawled and scratched
out entries
my life's journal
has always read only one line.

I am already inside
what I thought I had to strive for
What I was trying to pull myself up over the sheer cliff
wall for
I am already on the inside.
The heart beating
beating inside
is also the outside of us.

Dreams

PART ONE: *The Forming*

"You have a million dollars," I said
to her exasperatedly
I know in this economy
when you're old and your husband
needs care
it's not that much.
But let's face it—
It's not poor.

"When I was at Ohio State
unless a boy invited me out
on a Sunday night
I wouldn't eat dinner.
I didn't have any money
and the school
didn't serve
on Sunday nights
I was poor."

She used that word as if it wasn't the same word

We regularly use to describe
Demographics, neighborhoods, countries in the
developing world
It had some hidden meaning, some personal meaning
Some memory meaning
That made it sting more than the facts
Less than the circumstance
And beyond reparation.

She put herself through college
on a scholarship
the first in her immigrant family
to go to school. In nineteen-hundred
and fifty
that pretty much wasn't done,
unless you were a debutante
looking for a husband.
It wasn't really done
if your father was a night janitor in a grade school.

Her mother never knew
what she studied.
Being from the old school
it only mattered
what the sons did.

My grandfather used to collect the crayon stubs and
bring them to me
I filled milk cartons with ice cubes
Melted the colors, pouring them
Into a new mold
They were precious to me
until I grew up and found out where they came from—
Then they were sad.

PART TWO: *The Promise*

She went on to Chicago U
with the famed
and oh-so-arrogant
Bruno Bettleheim, who used the work
of his graduate students
as his own.
In college, I read his *Children of the Dream,*
and wondered how he could judge
kids from a radical social experiment
without even speaking the language—
but he did (or at least he published
about it) By then
I was already searching, wondering

how you go about
building a dream
And who might have
Real answers.

My mother was ahead of her times.
She wasn't a radical or a leftist,
If you saw her, you'd think
She was a most ordinary tollhouse cookie mom
Warm tomato soup, cheese sandwiches cut
In triangle quarters.
But she thought about things.
In an invisible way
not exactly following
a dream but more than just
being carried with the tides,
She was always deliberate.
She moved to New York City,
roommates with the late
M. S., the first woman newscaster
on a prime network,
her son now broadcasts for CNN,
you would know him
if I told you who he was.

She went to hear Dr. King preach in Harlem
with my father and a Chinese-American friend,
they were the only non-negro people
in the pews.
She hadn't remembered to tell me
until some fifty years later.
I guess it hadn't seemed significant to her
I wish I had known back when,
I might have asked her
What were you following?
I guess she didn't know
or she would have said

She and my father
moved in together—before they were married
They were handsome and pretty
in a fifties sort of way,
and free.
'It was so expensive in Manhattan'
she explained, 'it just made sense.
Dad was in school, we were poor'
I don't think she knew,
She was way ahead of her time.

She did things,

unexpected things
for the daughter of an immigrant family.
Though she never saw it that way.
She did a lot of things,
Though she could have done more.
I try to ask her
Even after all these years I still can't tell
if she was clutching after
the smoke curl of a dream
or if she just felt the waving
of the breeze

PART THREE: *The Meantime*

She furnished their first home,
on a young professor's salary
which was hardly anything, even then
she bought a coffee table
sturdy enough for toddlers to climb all over,
watching Mr. Rogers, all black and white,
zip his sweater.
he did, in fact, live in the neighborhood,
some eight blocks away. The coffee table was a small
fortune,

a little over a hundred fifty dollars,
'We were poor, 'she told me, 'but I found it
in an American Craftsman magazine
and we drove all the way to New Hope, PA.'
Little did she know or did she
The table carried in it the DNA of spiritual unfolding
The woodworker, a very early 1935 disciple of the great
Aurobindo Ghose.

PART FOUR: *Looking Back*

My husband and I used to be just as poor
But it didn't seem poor
We always felt rich
Just without the money
We had a dream.
When the scaffolding of that dream
summarily collapsed
into dirt and broken shards
we were able to move on.
If you really have a dream you can be rich
In the midst of the dust.

Now my mother has a million dollars
A little less every month

As my father's nursing eats it up, chunk by chunk
Still she has enough,
To live a chapter of a dream
If only she wouldn't endlessly worry
endlessly
emptying
One shelf at a time
Getting ready

She still is busy with the little things,
With what you do when you put life in order
The things you do in order to justify putting time
into your dream,
It's just that those little things have a way
of becoming the whole thing
till there's no time left
and misty eyed we start looking
towards the horizon
toward that chasm between this life
and the dream
of whatever comes
next.

PART FIVE: *Requiem*

Sometimes I try to catch
the wisp of the tail
of her tiger life
solitary and regal,
endangered and hungry.
Sometimes I catch myself
putting things in order
before putting treadle to my dream
even though, like her, no one's watching
no one's stopping
no one's saying
what I need to do.

When our time is our own
Will we make it what it could be,
in this life, now
not the next?

You never get ready for dreams
You take them by the horns and live them
Or hypnotize them with a whisper and climb on their
backs
It's not money or desperation

or spunk or freedom that makes people dream.
You can have courage, lots of it, and freedom and grit
Some selves aren't ready
to release their dream
From the spores in the soul
where the dreams rest
Until that time
for some unexpected reason they burst
Into being.

Be happy if you dream
If it takes you blind by the scruff of the neck
through this life
Through morning coffee
And afternoon haze
Through decades of seeking
And moments of rest
Through clearlight visions
And dull dead ends
Through desire and frustration
And love
And love
And love

Don't leave your dreams while you live in the meantime
Because you're poor
Or preparing
Or deliberate
Or sad
Or just too busy
putting
little things
into order.

Refusing to be Finished

Deep down inside   *I*

Gurgle with the primordial stew, fragments of life,
small strands floating in ether or essence, spirella that
drift and twitch blindly, occasionally bumping into each
other and fusing, merging, creating new forks and
strands and tendrils.

Deep down inside   *I*

Foment with the churn of the worlds, of all the winds
and waters, the humors and the chaff, swirling and
kneading until from the mouth of the cave form or
substance spew forth sometimes beauteous, sometimes
terrifying, sometimes ephemeral as smoke wisps or dust
lifted by an updraft to scatter across the waters below.

Deep down inside   *I*

Love with the oily wetness of lambswool, earthy and
pungent, nomads laying pelt tarps to bottom their

tents, opening to travellers and wanderers, magicians,
magi and me.

Deep down inside   *I*

Rest with the peace of the waters come to stillness from
the rocking of the earth, still, not without movement or
cessation of life, still as pregnancy, still as the fullness
and saturation of the circle of ink that makes for a full
stop.

Deep down inside   *I*

Breathe with the accordion fan, in and out, in and out,
bellows blowing sparks into life, music and sounds of
instruments and earth.

Deep down inside   *I*

Wonder at the next step, what wind the rivulet will take
around rock and jagged bend, over flat cliff face,
merging into marsh, feeding cattails and swampgrass
that blow and blow and bow in the wind?

Deep down inside   I

Move supple as a leaf, heavy as a buffalo, wise as a
whale that floats and waits, so large and so small in the
vast connected waterways of discovery.

Deep down inside   I

Sink below the surface of mind, below the objects that
move around in the pattern of my life—child, youth,
wanderer, yogi, taught now teacher.

Deep down inside   I

Sink in the midst of a sentence that refuses to be
finished

ABOUT THE AUTHOR

Amy Edelstein, educator, author, and public speaker is a powerful communicator of ideas and beliefs that can help us transform ourselves and the culture we live in. Amy is actively working to inspire people to discover the depths of the human heart and understand the complexity of a developmental context so we can create a beautiful and as yet unimagined culture. In 2014 she founded the nonprofit *Inner Strength Foundation*, which now works with over eight hundred inner city adolescents teaching mindfulness and a developmental perspective. Amy also cofounded *Emergence Education* in 2012 with her husband philosopher and spiritual teacher Jeff Carreira, which produces transformational programming and publications for an international audience. Amy has thirty-five years experience of contemplative practice, including a background in both Western and Eastern spiritual traditions, as well as in evolutionary spirituality. In recognition of her decades of indepth work in contemporary spirituality, collective emergence and cultural development, she was ordained the firstinterfaith minister of Evolutionary Spirituality and named its Wisdom Chair by the American Council of

Interfaith Churches. Amy is also author of *Love, Marriage & Evolution, Great Awakenings: Radical Visions of Spiritual Love & Evolution, Inner Strength Teen Program Teacher's Manual.* When not writing or teaching, Amy loves walking the streets of Philadelphia, contemplating cultural transformation, inspired by the spirit of our nation's early visionaries.

For more on Amy's books & trainings visit

www.AmyEdelstein.com

www.ingramcontent.com/pod-product-compliance
Lightning Source LLC
Chambersburg PA
CBHW051045030426
42339CB00006B/209